GAMEWORKS

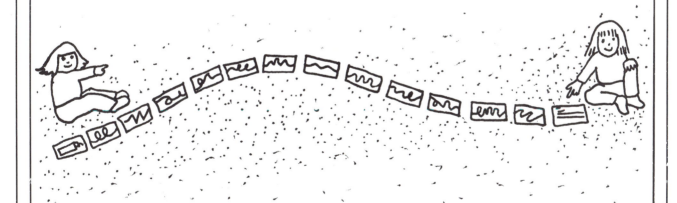

By Harriet Hodgson

Illustrated by Beth Savage

Cheryl McLain

Publisher: Roberta Suid
Editor: Elizabeth Russell
Cover Design: David Hale
Design and Production: Susan Pinkerton
Cover Art: Corbin Hillam

ISBN 0-912107-41-3

Monday Morning is a registered trademark
of Monday Morning Books, Inc.

Portions of this book were previously
published as *I Made It Myself!*

Printed in the United States of America

9 8 7 6 5 4 3 2 1

Contents

Introduction

Gameworks shows children how to create their own fun. This book is full of ideas for creative projects which children can make quickly and easily with free or inexpensive household materials, and minimal adult supervision. Children have fun making their own games, playing with them, and inventing new ways to use them. They also develop small motor coordination and thinking skills as they enjoy these activities.

GATHERING MATERIALS

The materials needed for each project are listed at the top of each page. They are recycleable throwaways and common items found around the house. Equipment needs are also simple — pencils, ballpoint pens, scissors, white glue, markers, string.

Collect all kinds of plastic, paper, styrofoam, and cardboard packaging materials. Wash and dry plastic bottles and tubs, shake crumbs from boxes, and fold paper bags. Check all items for safety. Do not use metal cans with sharp edges, containers which once held chemicals, or anything made of glass. Sort all materials and store in a handy place.

MAKING THE GAMES

Before doing any activity with children, make and play each game yourself to discover any difficulties with the project. You will also be able to see possibilities for substituting materials or extending the activity. In addition, you will see ways to use each project to reinforce learning skills.

Have materials and equipment ready before you begin. Nothing is more frustrating than having to stop in the middle of a project to hunt for something. It is better to make substitutions for materials before starting an activity.

Demonstrate the right way to use equipment. For example, use permanent markers in a well-ventilated room. Never allow children to sniff the fumes, as they can cause brain damage.

Show children the basic steps to make a game, but encourage them to use their imaginations to modify the games in any way they like. Children may want to design their games differently or make up different rules. Allow experimentation to extend each activity.

ENJOYING THE GAMES

Half the fun of these games is in the making. If part of a game is lost or broken, children can easily make another to replace it. The ideas in this book should also spark children's imaginations to invent new games of their own with materials they find around them.

Gameworks provides enjoyment for teachers, too. Materials needed are cheap and plentiful, and directions are simple enough for children to follow with little help. Motivation is built into the games themselves, and projects build many learning skills. For example, Alpha-Circles help very young children recognize letters, and Alphabetter reinforces spelling skills. Macaroni Match and Funny Fences give children practice in sequencing, while Eggs Plus reviews arithmetic. *Gameworks* combines crafts fun, games, and learning to brighten any day.

Alphabetter

WHAT YOU NEED:
Alphabet cereal
Large margarine tub
Plastic coffee scoop (or 1 tablespoon)
3-minute timer
Pencil
Paper

WHAT YOU DO:
1. Pour some cereal into the margarine tub.
2. Each player takes one scoop of cereal and spreads it out in front of him or her.
3. One player starts the timer and says, "Go." Each player makes as many words as possible in three minutes.
4. Keep score with pencil and paper, counting one point for each letter used. Words of eight letters or more count double.
5. The player with the highest score wins. All players get to eat some cereal.

Alpha-Circles

WHAT YOU NEED:
26 tops from gallon-size plastic milk bottles
3 egg cartons
Marker

WHAT YOU DO:
1. Print one alphabet letter on each clean, dry bottle top with the marker to make alpha-circles.
2. Cut the lids off two egg cartons, leaving the third one whole.
3. Print one alphabet letter in the bottom of each compartment in the egg cartons. The third egg carton will have only y and z.
4. Put each alpha-circle on top of the letter it matches in the egg cartons.
5. Make words on table top with alpha-circles.

Animal Crackers

WHAT YOU NEED:
Box of animal crackers
Pencil
Scissors
White glue
Paper
Spring-type wooden clothespins
Margarine tubs

WHAT YOU DO:
1. Trace around each animal shape on a piece of paper.
2. Cut out paper animal shapes and paste each on the end of a clothespin.
3. Snap each clothespin onto a margarine tub to show where crackers go.
4. Sort the rest of the crackers into the right margarine tubs.

Apple Basket

WHAT YOU NEED:
Lids from peel-strip juice cans
Pencil
Permanent markers
Large piece of cardboard
1 die
Margarine tub with lid

WHAT YOU DO:
1. Use one lid as a pattern to draw a row of circles that curves from one edge of the cardboard to the other.
2. Draw stems and leaves on the circles to make them look like apples.
3. Draw an arrow in the first circle to mark the start of the game. Draw a basket in the last circle to mark the end of the game.
4. Code each juice can lid with a different color marker. Use the lids as playing pieces. Put the die in the margarine tub and snap on the lid.
5. Take turns shaking the die. Move each playing piece forward the number of spaces shown on the die. The first player to reach the basket is the winner.

Beautiful Buttons

WHAT YOU NEED:
Egg carton
Crayons
Old buttons

WHAT YOU DO:
1. Color each egg carton compartment a different color.
2. Use the carton two ways. First, collect old buttons and pop them into the compartments with matching colors.
3. Second, play a button flip game. Players get equal numbers of buttons. Standing back from the egg carton, players take turns flipping buttons into it. Score one point for each button landing in a compartment. Score an extra point for each button which lands in a matching color compartment.

Berry Basket Bounce

WHAT YOU NEED:
Berry baskets (1 per player)
Small ball

WHAT YOU DO:
1. Players take turns bouncing the ball and catching it in the basket. Each successful catch earns another try.
2. Player with the most catches in a row is the winner.
3. Make the game harder by changing the rules to catching the ball after two or three bounces.

Bottle Bowling

WHAT YOU NEED:
Empty detergent bottles (all the same size)
Ball

WHAT YOU DO:
1. Set up the clean, dry bottles on the floor like bowling pins.
2. Roll the ball to knock down as many balls as possible.

Button and Cup

WHAT YOU NEED:
Styrofoam cup
Nail
Large button
String

WHAT YOU DO:
1. Punch a hole with the nail close to the rim of the styrofoam cup.
2. Tie one end of the string to the cup and the other end to a large button.
3. Swing the string slowly and catch the button in the cup. Don't make the string too long or it might hit someone.

Button Winks

WHAT YOU NEED:
Paper plate
Marker
Crayons
Old buttons

WHAT YOU DO:
1. Draw three concentric circles on the paper plate.
2. Print "10" on the smallest circle, "5" on the middle circle, and "1" on the largest circle. These are the points scored.
3. Color the circles.
4. Find flat old buttons. Be sure they can be flipped like tiddly winks.
5. Place the plate on the rug. Players take turns flipping buttons toward the plate. The player with the highest score wins.

Cake Bake

WHAT YOU NEED:
Colored paper
Pencil
Scissors
Square cake pan

WHAT YOU DO:
1. Trace around the bottom of the cake pan on the colored paper.
2. Cut out the square to fit in the pan.
3. Cut the square into puzzle pieces.
4. Work the square puzzle in the pan.

Canned Consonants

WHAT YOU NEED:
Coffee can
Plastic coffee can lids
Ball-point pen
Small household objects

WHAT YOU DO:
1. Print a consonant letter on each coffee can lid.
2. Search around for small things that begin with that letter. Put them all in the can and snap on the lid. Shake them up, dump them out, and do it again with another lid.
3. Try the same thing with vowels.

Catch-Ball

WHAT YOU NEED:
Plastic milk bottles
Kitchen shears
Ball

WHAT YOU DO:
1. Cut the bottom off each plastic milk bottle, slanting upward toward the handle, as shown. Leave the handle on to make a catching scoop.
2. Use the scoops to play catch with the ball. If no ball is handy, throw and catch a sponge.
3. More than two people can play. The faster the game, the better.

Cereal Box Puzzles

WHAT YOU NEED:
Empty cereal boxes
Scissors
Crayons
Envelopes

WHAT YOU DO:
1. Cut the front off each cereal box carefully.
2. Cut the box front into puzzle shapes.
3. Color code the puzzle pieces on the back to prevent mixups.
   Keep each puzzle in its own envelope.
4. Make mini puzzles from small cereal and pudding boxes.

Chippers

WHAT YOU NEED:
Brown paper bags
Scissors
Margarine tub
Small piece of cardboard
Nail or nutpick
Brass paper fastener
Large safety pin
Potato chip cannisters (1 per player)

WHAT YOU DO:
1. Cut lots of circles from paper bags to make "potato chips." Store all the chips in the margarine tub.
2. Draw a circle on the cardboard and print the numerals from 0 through 9 around the edge of the circle, using 0 several times.
3. Poke a hole in the center of the circle with a nail or nutpick. Slip the brass paper fastener through the end of the safety pin and put it through the center hole in the circle to make a game spinner.
4. Players take turns spinning the spinner and dropping the number of chips indicated into their cannisters. If a player spins a 0, all the chips are dumped out and the player begins again.
5. The first player to get 50 "potato chips" wins.

Clippety-Snippety

WHAT YOU NEED:
Large brown envelope
Pen
Colored paper
Scrap paper
Scissors
Paste

WHAT YOU DO:
1. Print the names of the different ways to cut paper with scissors on the outside of the envelope. Examples: fringing, straight, folded, etc.
2. Make a sample of each kind of cutting with colored paper. Example: a valentine for folded cutting.
3. Paste each sample of cutting by its name as a reminder.
4. Store scissors and scrap paper in the envelope. Use Clippety-Snippety when in the mood for cutting — great for rainy days.

Clothespin Drop

WHAT YOU NEED:
Plastic milk bottle
Kitchen shears
Clothespins

WHAT YOU DO:
1. Cut a hole in the top of the plastic milk bottle, but leave the handle on.
2. Stand over the milk carton with legs straight. Drop clothespins through the hole.
3. Store clothespins in the milk bottle.

Clothespin Words

WHAT YOU NEED:
Spring-type wooden clothespins
Wire hanger
Permanent marker

WHAT YOU DO:
1. Print an alphabet letter on each clothespin. Include both vowels and consonants.
2. Snap clothespins to hanger to make as many words as possible.
3. One or more can play. Players can time each other to see how many words they can make in a minute.

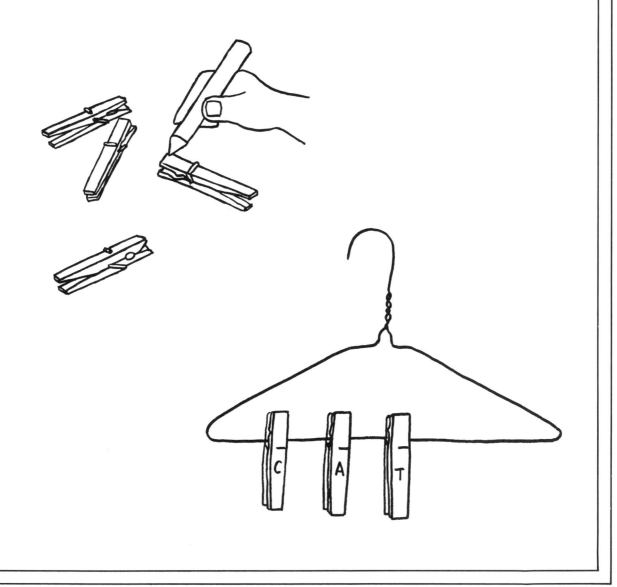

Cockeyed Comics

WHAT YOU NEED:
Newspaper comics
Scissors
Paper
Paste

WHAT YOU DO:
1. Cut one comic strip apart.
2. Paste the comic squares on paper, one per page. Scramble them.
3. Play three ways: Look at the pictures and put the story back together; read the words and put the story back together; or mix up the pictures and tell a cockeyed story to go with them.

Cylinder Ball

WHAT YOU NEED:
Large cardboard ice cream bucket (from ice cream store)
Kitchen shears
Nails with flat heads
Hammer
Ball, sponge, or knotted sock

WHAT YOU DO:
1. Cut the bottom out of the ice cream bucket to make a cylinder.
2. Nail the cylinder to a tree or post. Use it like a basketball hoop with a ball, sponge, or knotted sock.

Detective

WHAT YOU NEED:
Plastic lid
Scissors
Spring-type clothespin

WHAT YOU DO:
1. Cut out the center from the plastic lid, leaving the rim.
2. Snap the clothespin onto the ring to make a handle.
3. Pretend the ring is a magnifying glass and use it to search for things that are the same color, things that are rough or smooth, or things that rhyme.

Don't Tickle a Trout

WHAT YOU NEED:
Cardboard
Crayons
Scissors
2 shoelaces

WHAT YOU DO:
1. Draw a big fish shape on the cardboard.
2. Put the fish on the floor and place a shoelace on each side.
3. Players jump across the shoelace "brook" without falling in. Each time a player jumps, the shoelaces are moved farther apart.
4. The last one to make a good jump is the winner.

Eggs Plus

WHAT YOU NEED:
Plastic pantyhose egg
Permanent marker
Paper

WHAT YOU DO:
1. Open the egg and print a numeral on the outside of the smaller half.
2. Print numerals on the outside of the larger half to make number problems. Examples: +2, +4, +6.
3. Print the same number problems and their answers on the paper. Hide the paper inside the egg.
4. Slowly turn the egg and line up the numerals. Add numbers together, then check answers.
5. Make other eggs for subtracting or multiplying.

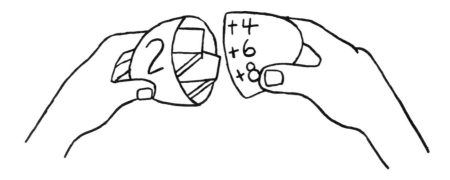

Four Score

WHAT YOU NEED:
Paper
Pencil
1 die
Margarine tub with lid

WHAT YOU DO:
1. Draw six squares at the top of a piece of paper. Draw dots in the squares to make them look like the sides of dice. This paper becomes a score card. Make one for each player.
2. Put the die in the margarine tub and snap on the lid.
3. Players take turns shaking the die and marking an X under the matching dot picture on the scorecard.
4. The first player to get four of a kind is the winner.

Funny Fences

WHAT YOU NEED:
Egg carton
Paper
Scissors
Crayons
Colored plastic spring-type clothespins

WHAT YOU DO:
1. Cut the paper in pieces to fit inside the egg carton. These are code cards.
2. Color the code cards. Draw straight lines on pieces of paper in colors that match the clothespins. Example: two green lines, three red, four blue, and two green. Make lots of code cards.
3. Open the egg carton. Put one code card inside the lid.
4. Build a fence of clothespins to follow the code card. Match a red clothespin to a red line, a yellow clothespin to a yellow line, etc.
5. Players can time themselves to see how fast they can build a fence and take it down.

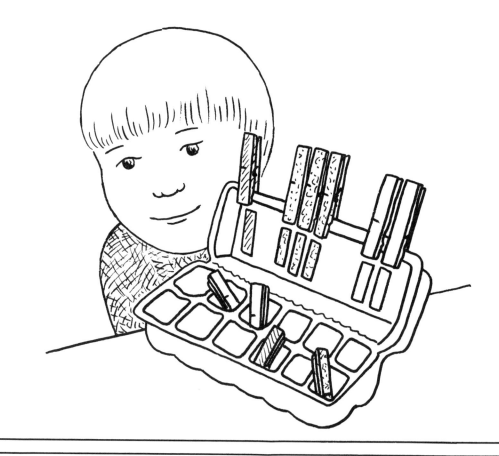

Gone Fishin'

WHAT YOU NEED:
Paper
Scissors
Crayon
Paper punch
Paper clips
Pencil
String
Magnet
Plastic ice cream bucket

WHAT YOU DO:
1. Draw lots of fish shapes on paper and cut them out.
2. Draw a circle, triangle, rectangle, or square on each fish.
3. Punch a hole in each fish and put a paper clip through each hole.
4. Put the fish in the bucket and mix them up.
5. Tie the magnet onto the string. Tie the string onto the pencil to make a fishing pole.
6. Players take turns fishing for just one shape. Store fish and pole in bucket.

How Long?

WHAT YOU NEED:
Tape measure
Old magazines
Scissors
Paste
File cards

WHAT YOU DO:
1. Cut out magazine pictures of things to measure.
2. Paste one picture on each file card. Mix up all the cards.
3. Players take turns closing eyes and picking a card, then going and measuring that object. Each player writes the length on the card.
4. Play continues until all cards are gone.

Jumpscotch

WHAT YOU NEED:
Large plastic trash bag
Permanent marker
Masking tape

WHAT YOU DO:
1. Lay the trash bag flat on the floor. Divide the bag into seven spaces with the marker. Draw a large rectangle across the top and two columns of three squares below it.
2. Draw arrows going around the bag, with one big arrow in each box.
3. Tape jumpscotch to the floor to prevent slipping.
4. Players play barefoot.

Learn-to-Button Animals

WHAT YOU NEED:
Animal patterns
Tracing paper
Felt
Pins or tape
Ball-point pen
Needle
Scissors
Thread
Buttons

WHAT YOU DO:
1. Trace the animal patterns on the next page and cut out.
2. Place the patterns on felt, using a different color for each animal. Pin or tape down the patterns. Trace around each pattern with a ball-point pen.
3. Cut out the felt shapes. Cut button holes in the felt as shown.
4. Sew buttons on shapes where indicated.
5. Use the animals in three ways: button them together; match colors; or invent crazy, mixed-up animals.

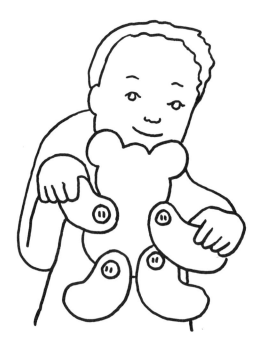

Lid Toss

WHAT YOU NEED:
5 plastic lids (same size)
Scissors
Pencil
Cardboard tube from paper towels
Margarine tub

WHAT YOU DO:
1. Cut the centers from the plastic lids and save the rings.
2. Trace the circumference of the cardboard tube on the bottom of the margarine tub and cut out.
3. Turn the margarine tub upside down. Push the tube into the hole.
4. Players toss the rings over the tube, scoring one point for each ringer.

Little Bubbles

WHAT YOU NEED:
Spring-type clothespin
Spice bottle top with holes
Liquid detergent
Margarine tub

WHAT YOU DO:
1. Clip the clothespin onto the spice bottle top.
2. Pour some detergent into the margarine tub and dip in the top.
3. Hold the clothespin handle and blow through the holes in the bottle top.

Lunchbox

WHAT YOU NEED:
Old magazines
Scissors
Paste
Index cards
Old lunchbox

WHAT YOU DO:
1. Cut out magazine pictures of food and objects.
2. Paste pictures onto index cards. Be sure the cards fit into the lunchbox.
3. Mix up the cards and sort the pictures. Only the food pictures go into the lunchbox.

Macaroni Match

WHAT YOU NEED:
2 kinds of macaroni for stringing
Shoelace
Bowl
Index cards
Pencil

WHAT YOU DO:
1. Put the macaroni in the bowl and mix well.
2. Knot the shoelace at one end.
3. Draw pictures on the index cards of different patterns for stringing macaroni. Example: two straight noodles, three round, two straight, etc. These are code cards.
4. Follow one code card at a time and string macaroni on the shoelace to match the pattern shown.
5. Tie the ends of the shoelace together to make a necklace or bracelet out of an especially nice macaroni pattern.

Marble Track

WHAT YOU NEED:
Cardboard tubes from paper towels
Scissors
Glue
Paper punch
String
Marbles

WHAT YOU DO:
1. Cut the cardboard tubes in half lengthwise.
2. Glue the tubes together at the ends to form a long track.
3. Punch a hole at one end of the track. Tie a string handle through the hole.
4. Hook the track onto a door knob and roll marbles down it.
5. Try aiming marbles at a target like an ice cream bucket lying on its side.

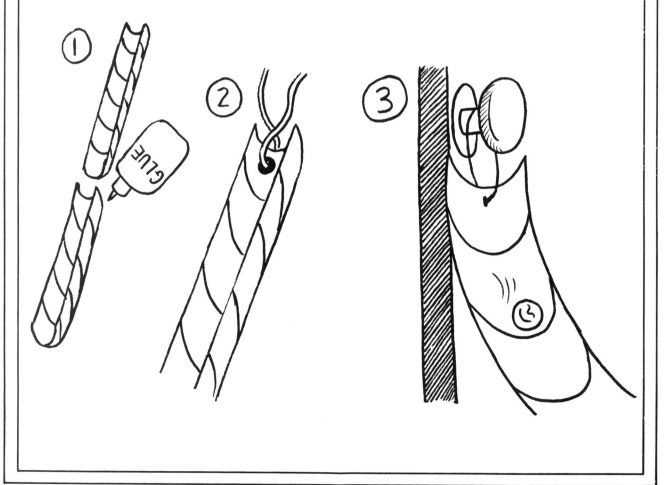

Musical Door Hook

WHAT YOU NEED:
Large metal door hook
Shoelace
Nail

WHAT YOU DO:
1. Buy the biggest metal door hook available at a hardware store.
2. Tie the shoelace onto the hook.
3. Hit the hook with the nail to make a sound like a triangle.
4. Tap out the rhythm to a song and have others guess what it is.

Name Worm

WHAT YOU NEED:
Paper
Pencil
Scissors

WHAT YOU DO:
1. Draw a fat, wiggly worm shape on paper. Draw an eye and a mouth at the left, as shown.
2. Print name on the worm, leaving a space between each letter.
3. Cut the worm into puzzle pieces.
4. Put the name worm puzzle back together.
5. Make lots of name worms, each on a different color paper. Store them all in a can for a "can of worms."

Nothing-to-Do Cards

WHAT YOU NEED:
Index cards
Pencil
Paper punch
Yarn or string

WHAT YOU DO:
1. Print one thing that is fun to do on each card. Examples: looking at books, baking cookies, watering plants, building with blocks.
2. Punch a hole at the top of each index card.
3. Tie all the cards together and save.
4. When there seems to be nothing to do, close eyes and pick a card.

Number Snap

WHAT YOU NEED:
Cereal box
Scissors
Permanent marker
Spring-type wooden clothespins

WHAT YOU DO:
1. Cut the back off the box.
2. Print numerals on both sides of the clothespins.
3. Write number series in the bottom of the cereal box.
4. Use the bottom of the box as a clothespin stand. Snap different number series onto it. Examples: count by twos, snap two odd and one even number, etc.

Pumpkin Pinata

WHAT YOU NEED:
Paper bag
Crayons or markers
Newspaper
Small prizes (balloons, lollipops, etc.)
String
Scissors
Blindfold
Wooden spoon

WHAT YOU DO:
1. Draw a jack-o-lantern face on one side of the bag.
2. Wad newspaper into balls. Stuff the bag with newspaper and prizes.
3. Cut a piece of string about two feet long. Tie the bag closed with one end of the string and make a loop handle on the other end.
4. Hang the pinata in a safe place.
5. Each player is blindfolded and tries to hit the pinata with the wooden spoon to release the prizes.

Rhymers

WHAT YOU NEED:
Egg carton
Ball-point pen
Button

WHAT YOU DO:
1. Print word endings in some of the compartments of the egg carton. Examples: ___at, ___an, ___un.
2. Draw a smiling face in each of the blank spaces.
3. Put the button in the egg carton and close the lid.
4. Shake the carton and open the lid. If the button lands on an ending, think of as many words as possible that rhyme with that ending.
5. If the button lands on a smiling face, clap and try again.

Ring-O

WHAT YOU NEED:
Plastic lid
Scissors
Cardboard tube from paper towels
Paper punch
String

WHAT YOU DO:
1. Cut out the inside of a plastic lid to make a ring.
2. Punch a hole at one end of the cardboard tube. Tie the plastic ring onto the tube with a 12″ length of string.
3. Swing the ring slowly and catch it on the tube.

Sand Pendulum

WHAT YOU NEED:
Plastic detergent bottle
Kitchen shears
Paper punch
String
Sand or uncooked rice

WHAT YOU DO:
1. Cut the bottom off the detergent bottle, saving the top.
2. Punch two holes on opposite sides of the cut edge.
3. Cut a length of string and tie it through the holes for a handle.
4. Fill the pendulum with sand or dry, uncooked rice.
5. Hold the pendulum in one hand and set it swinging with the other. Predict what kinds of shapes it will make.

Shadow Puppets

WHAT YOU NEED:

Cookie cutters
Pencil
Paper
Scissors
Paper punch
Glue
Craft sticks

WHAT YOU DO:

1. Trace around the cookie cutters on paper.
2. Cut out the paper shapes. Punch eyes where needed with the paper punch.
3. Glue shapes onto craft sticks.
4. Make up stories and act them out with shadow puppets indoors with a flashlight or outdoors in the sun.

Shape Sorting

WHAT YOU NEED:
Coffee can with plastic lid
Scissors
Ball-point pen
Tops from plastic milk bottles
Large sponge
Clothespins

WHAT YOU DO:
1. Cut the sponge into squares.
2. Use the pen to trace a clothespin, a sponge square, and a bottle top on the coffee can lid.
3. Cut the shapes from the lid.
4. Push all objects through the matching holes. Store all game parts right in the can.

Silly Eggs

WHAT YOU NEED:
4 plastic pantyhose eggs
Paper
Crayons
Scissors

WHAT YOU DO:
1. Draw four egg pictures on paper with crayons. Draw scrambled eggs, fried eggs, bacon and eggs, and boiled eggs.
2. Cut each picture into puzzle pieces.
3. Code all puzzle pieces to prevent mix-ups. Put a "B" on the backs of the pieces of the boiled egg picture, an "F" on the backs of the pieces of the fried egg picture, etc.
4. Put a puzzle inside each egg.
5. Choose an egg. Shake it, then work the puzzle.

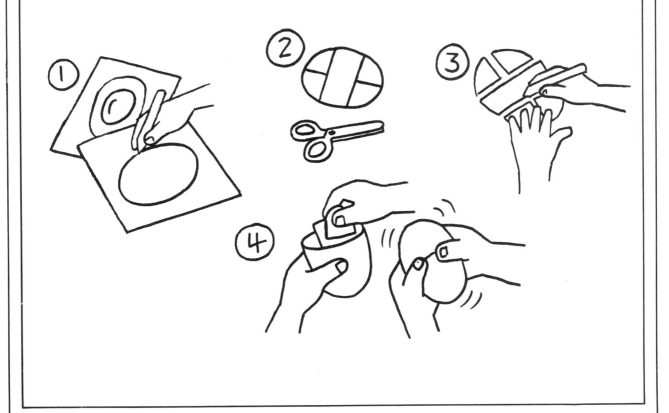

Stickeroo

WHAT YOU NEED:
Styrofoam meat trays
Nail
Pencil or pen
Long shoelace

WHAT YOU DO:
1. Print a large numeral or letter on the outside bottom of each meat tray.
2. Poke some holes along the lines with the nail. Leave space between the holes.
3. Knot one end of the shoelace so that it doesn't pull out. Stitch along each number or letter card.

Stitcheroo

WHAT YOU NEED:
Shallow box with lid
Pencil
Flannel
Felt
Scissors
Glue

WHAT YOU DO:
1. Trace the box lid on the flannel and cut out.
2. Glue the flannel rectangle inside the lid.
3. Cut a variety of shapes from felt.
4. Make pictures by pressing the shapes to the flannel.
5. Tell a story to go with each picture.

Story Spinner

WHAT YOU NEED:
Scissors
Old magazines
Paste
Nail
Brass paper fastener
Diaper pin or large paper clip
Cardboard pizza tray (from frozen pizza)

WHAT YOU DO:
1. Cut out pictures from magazines.
2. Paste pictures around the pizza tray.
3. Punch a hole in the center of the circle with the nail.
4. Fasten a diaper pin or a large paper clip to the center of the circle with the brass paper fastener to make the game spinner.
5. Twirl the spinner and tell a story including each picture it points to.
6. Make a second story spinner on the other side of the cardboard pizza tray.

Swinging Snowman

WHAT YOU NEED:
Paper plate
Scissors
Cardboard toilet paper tube
Crayons
Colored paper scrap
Glue
Margarine tub lids
Yarn
2 spring-type clothespins (optional)

WHAT YOU DO:
1. Cut out the center of the paper plate and save for the face.
2. Trace the circumference of the tube on the face and cut out. Fit the tube into the circle for a long nose. Draw eyes and mouth on the face.
3. Cut a hat from the colored paper scrap and glue on the snowman's head. Glue the head onto the paper plate ring.
4. Cut a length of yarn to hang the snowman. Knot the ends and glue on the back.
5. Cut centers from clean margarine tub lids to form rings.
6. Hang the snowman in a doorway. Fling rings through the center and onto the nose. To make the game harder, clip two clothespin arms to the snowman and try to ring them too.

Target Toss

WHAT YOU NEED:
Large magazine or newspaper picture
Paste
Cardboard
Marker
Ball, sponge, or knotted sock

WHAT YOU DO:
1. Cut out a large picture from a magazine or newspaper. Paste the picture onto the cardboard to make the target.
2. Print numerals on different parts of the target to tell points scored.
3. Players take turns throwing the ball at the target. Player with the highest score wins. Make the game harder by standing farther back.

Tell A Yarn

WHAT YOU NEED:
Yarn
Small prize

WHAT YOU DO:
1. Tie the prize to one end of the yarn.
2. Wind the yarn around the prize into a ball and knot the end.
3. Players sit in a circle. One person holds the knot and starts a story. Each player unwinds a bit of the yarn while adding to the story. Players hold onto yarn and pass the ball on.
4. The person at the end of the yarn gets to keep the prize and end the story.

Terrific Target

WHAT YOU NEED:
Plastic lid
Notched garbage bag tie
Nail
Ball, sponge, or knotted sock

WHAT YOU DO:
1. Poke a hole near the edge of the lid with the nail.
2. Push the garbage bag tie through the hole and fasten it together to make a hanger.
3. Hang the target anywhere. Throw the ball, sponge, or knotted sock at the target. Water pistols work well too — outside.

Tic-Tac Tops

WHAT YOU NEED:
10 plastic milk bottle tops
Permanent marker
Paper

WHAT YOU DO:
1. Draw X's on five of the tops and O's on the other five tops.
2. Draw tic-tac-toe lines on a piece of paper.
3. Players see who can win three out of five games, or five out of seven games.

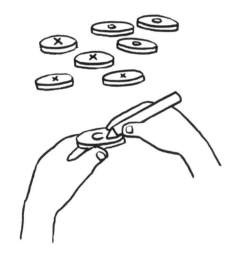

Toothpaste

WHAT YOU NEED:
Magazine picture of toothpaste
Magazine picture of a toothbrush
Scissors
Paste
Index cards
Marker

WHAT YOU DO:
1. Cut out the magazine pictures. Paste them onto index cards.
2. Draw all sorts of lines on blank index cards starting at one edge of a card and ending at another edge.
3. Lay the toothpaste card on the floor. Then lay the line cards down, connecting the lines to show the path the toothpaste takes.
4. Lay down the toothbrush card at the end of the toothpaste path.

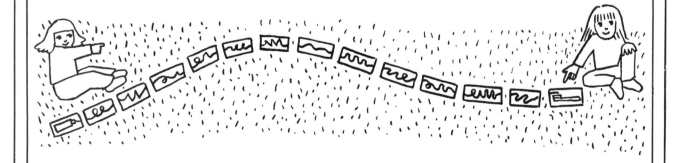

Tough Puzzle

WHAT YOU NEED:
2 identical magazine pictures
Paper
Glue
Scissors

WHAT YOU DO:
1. Cut out the magazine pictures.
2. Glue pictures on paper.
3. Cut one of the pictures into tricky puzzle shapes.
4. Work the "tough puzzle" on top of the whole picture.

Vegetable Soup

WHAT YOU NEED:
Small saucepan
Paper
Pencil
Old magazines
Scissors
Paste

WHAT YOU DO:
1. Trace the bottom of the saucepan on paper to make many circles. Cut out all the circles.
2. Cut out magazine pictures of all kinds of food.
3. Paste each food picture on a paper circle and mix them up.
4. Sort pictures of vegetables into the pan to make "vegetable soup."

Whirl-O

WHAT YOU NEED:
String
Button
Scissors
Crepe paper, fat yarn, or ribbon for streamers

WHAT YOU DO:
1. Tie string on the button, leaving tails about a foot long.
2. Knot the streamers onto one tail near the button.
3. Hold onto the other tail. Swing the streamers in arcs, figure eights, circles — any way.

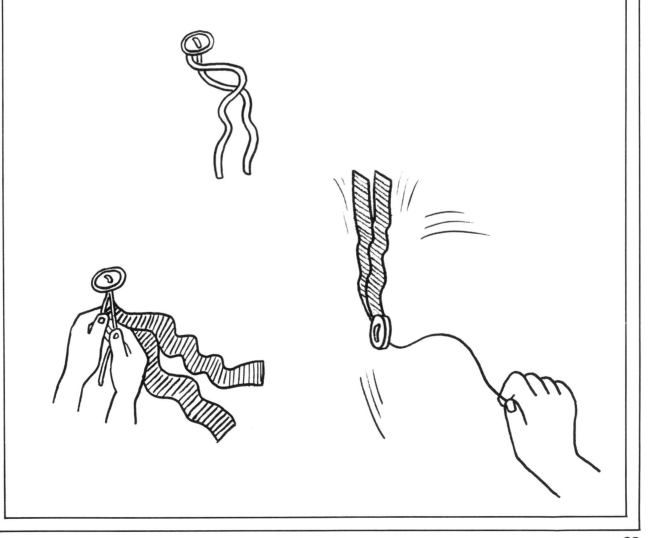

Writing Kit

WHAT YOU NEED:
Pencil
Eraser
Plain paper
Watercolor pen
Sponge
Scissors
Coffee can with see-through plastic lid

WHAT YOU DO:
1. Put pencil, eraser, plain paper, watercolor pen, and sponge into the coffee can.
2. Cut out paper circles to fit inside the coffee can lid.
3. Print a capital and a small letter on each paper circle to make round alphabet cards.
4. Place the coffee can lid over a letter card. Trace the letter onto the lid with the watercolor pen.
5. Dampen the sponge and wipe the lid clean after tracing each set of letters.